Goddesses of Greek Mythology

Don Nardo

San Diego, CA

About the Author

Classical historian and award-winning author Don Nardo has written numerous acclaimed volumes about ancient civilizations and peoples. They include more than a dozen overviews of the mythologies of the Sumerians, Babylonians, Egyptians, Greeks, Romans, Persians, Celts, and others. Nardo, who also composes and arranges orchestral music, lives with his wife, Christine, in Massachusetts.

© 2020 ReferencePoint Press, Inc.
Printed in the United States

For more information, contact:
ReferencePoint Press, Inc.
PO Box 27779
San Diego, CA 92198
www.ReferencePointPress.com

LIBRARY OF CONGRESS CATALOGING-IN-PUBLICATION DATA

Name: Nardo, Don, 1947– author.
Title: Goddesses of Greek Mythology/by Don Nardo.
Description: San Diego: ReferencePoint Press, 2019. | Series: Exploring
  Greek Mythology | Includes bibliographical references and index.
Identifiers: LCCN 2018038093 (print) | LCCN 2018042288 (ebook) | ISBN
  9781682826249 (eBook) | ISBN 9781682826232 (hardback)
Subjects: LCSH: Goddesses, Greek.
Classification: LCC BL795.G63 (ebook) | LCC BL795.G63 N37 2019 (print) | DDC
  292.2/114—dc23
LC record available at https://lccn.loc.gov/2018038093

Contents

Introduction

Myths as Mangled Memories

Just about everyone is familiar with at least a few ancient Greek myths or the main characters in those stories. These tales—some exciting, others quaint, and still others mysterious or thought-provoking—have fascinated every succeeding generation within Western (European-based) civilization. Moreover, books, movies, video games, TV shows, and commercials continue to exploit the gods, heroes, monsters, and other facets of the vast collection of Greek myths.

The Heroic World

The natural first question that many people ask about these timeless tales is: Where did they come from? The answer, modern experts say, is that many, if not most, of the Greek myths were mangled memories of real people and events from a preclassical Greek civilization. Employed in a very general sense, the term *classical* here denotes the residents of the Greek-speaking lands from about 750 to 350 BCE. That was the period that produced great thinkers like Socrates, Plato, and Aristotle; the first true historians, Herodotus and Thucydides; and Athens's cultural golden age, in which democracy and the theater were invented and the famous Parthenon temple was erected.

What Aristotle and his contemporaries did not know but modern historians *do* know is that many centuries before classical Greece emerged, the Greek sphere was home to a different advanced civilization. It reached its height during the late Bronze Age, lasting from about 1600 to 1150 BCE. Two separate cultures thrived—one, the Minoan, was centered in Crete and other Aegean islands; the other, the Mycenaean, established small but powerful kingdoms on Greece's mainland. The Mycenaeans eventually conquered and absorbed the Minoans and flourished until their civilization collapsed, for reasons that are still not well understood, between 1200 and 1100 BCE.

Thereafter, the numerous imposing Bronze Age palaces and fortresses were abandoned, and reading and writing, the arts, and several other aspects of civilized society largely disappeared. Today historians call the three-century-long period that followed this collapse ancient Greece's Dark Age. During that period most Greeks were poor, illiterate farmers and herders who inhabited small villages or isolated islands.

As the decades and centuries elapsed, a kind of cultural amnesia about the lost Bronze Age world set in, and people more or less forgot their once illustrious heritage. Yet at least a few shreds of past glories were not forgotten. Dimly remembered and often twisted or exaggerated, they became the basis for a number of vibrant and romanticized tales. Eventually, when classical Greece arose from the cultural slumbers of the Dark Age, people attributed all those archaic stories to a period they called the Age of Heroes. The classical Greeks had no clear idea when that era had occurred. More important was that it seemed to have been a special, magical time. As the late, great scholar of ancient Greece C.M. Bowra put it, Plato and his peers "saw in this lost society something heroic and superhuman, which embodied an ideal of what men should be and do and suffer. Their imaginations, inflamed by ancient stories of vast undertakings and incomparable heroes, of gods walking on the earth as friends of men, [came together in] a vision of a heroic world."[1]

Ancient Greece (circa 500 BCE)

Awe and Respect

Those "gods walking on the earth" that Bowra mentioned were of two kinds—male and female. More to the point, their genders were not abstract or generalized but rather fully humanized in all respects. Indeed, the Greeks anthropomorphized their deities; i.e., envisioned them as both looking and acting like people. Furthermore, those divinities possessed a number of human passions, both positive and negative, as well as all manner of imperfections, which sets them apart from the deities of most other religions in history. Visualizing the gods this way made them seem more understandable and approachable, the late historian Michael Grant pointed out. "These gods and goddesses," he wrote, "are human beings writ large, because the Greeks, with their lively, dramatic, and plastic [flexible] sense, were so conscious of the potential of men and women that they could not imagine the deities in any other shape."[2]

Nevertheless, the Greeks were well aware that no matter how much gods and humans resembled each other, one crucial factor separated them. This was a vast disparity in power. "From a single mother," both deities and people "draw breath," the fifth-century-BCE Greek poet Pindar said. "But a difference of power in everything keeps us apart."[3]

Moreover, that this divine power manifested itself as much in goddesses as in male gods seemed exceptional. In classical Greek eyes, females were limited in power and inferior to men in all other aspects of nature. Greek society was highly

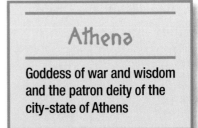

Athena

Goddess of war and wisdom and the patron deity of the city-state of Athens

patriarchal, or male dominated, with women uniformly treated as weaker than men and also legally and morally inferior to them. For a man to treat his wife and daughters as lesser beings and then turn around and literally worship a strong and resourceful goddess, such as the war-deity Athena, may sometimes have appeared unnatural.

Yet Greek men never doubted the importance of such worship. First, the goddesses supposedly wielded powers that overshadowed those of even the strongest human men. Second, the female deities had to be esteemed because they held the secrets of reproduction, one of the few aspects of life over which men had little or no control. As Norwegian scholar Evy J. Haland points out, male classical Greeks' fear of the very concept of powerful women was based more than anything else on men's "fear of women's reproductive power. Men wanted to rule that power [but] never managed to do so, simply because they belonged to another sex and did not know 'the female secrets.'"[4] For the classical Greeks, therefore, the goddesses and their traditional myths were simultaneously mysterious, awe-inspiring, and ultimately to be respected at all costs.

Chapter One

Guardians of Nature's Realm

"I begin to sing," an ancient Greek religious hymn opens, "of the glorious goddess, bright-eyed, inventive, unbending of heart, pure virgin, savior of cities, and courageous. [When she was born] great Olympus began to reel horribly at the might of the bright-eyed goddess and earth round about cried fearfully, and the sea was moved and tossed with dark waves, while foam burst forth suddenly."[5]

The "glorious goddess" the hymn describes was Athena, the principal Greek female deity of war and wisdom. According to the myth describing her birth, earth and sea trembled because she suddenly exploded outward, fully clad in her shining armor, from the head of her divine father, Zeus. Leader of the Olympian gods (the deities who dwelled atop Mount Olympus), he easily survived the trauma. But the world as a whole was shaken. In that incredible instant, Athena demonstrated that a goddess, no less than any of her male Olympian counterparts, could send shock waves blasting through nature's realm.

No less stunning was the fact that the war goddess did not even represent or oversee any of the world's natural features, such as the sky, oceans, fields, fire, storms, or rainbows. Other goddesses supervised, guarded, or personified those diverse aspects of nature. Without their divine influence on nature, the Greeks believed, humanity could not survive long, much less prosper. It was essential, therefore, for each human community to recognize those goddesses and appease them through regular worship.

The Indispensable Goddess

Most of the female deities were adored and honored by the classical Greeks, but Hestia held a special place in their hearts. A hymn to her that they frequently recited says in part, "In all the temples of the gods she has a share of honor."[6] This was not intended to suggest that Hestia was the strongest or most influential goddess. Rather, it was meant to indicate that she was the most indispensable, or necessary, of them.

The reason for Hestia's high status among the female deities was that she was in charge of fire, and in particular the fires that people used for warmth, cooking, and burning animals and plants in religious sacrifices. Put more concisely, she was goddess of the hearth. In that crucial role, she was the object of a family's first home sacrifice in a given day or week. The *prytaneum*, or communal hearth, of each Greek city-state was seen as a sacred shrine to her and her alone. Moreover, when a Greek community founded a colony in a foreign land, it brought embers from the mother *prytaneum* to ignite the new one.

Some idea of the tremendous respect the Greeks had for Hestia can be seen in a popular hymn that was often recited or sung in her honor. It said in part, "Hestia, in the high dwellings of all, both deathless gods and men who walk on earth, you have gained an everlasting abode and highest honor. Glorious is your portion and your right. For without you, mortals hold no banquet."[7] This acknowledged that without her maintenance of human hearths, people could not cook their food and behave as civilized beings set apart from mere animals, which consume raw meat.

One of Hestia's primary myths describes how she was the firstborn child of Cronos, leader of the first race of gods, the Titans. Her mother, and Cronos's mate, was Rhea. The crude and

A scene painted on a sixth-century BCE Greek vase shows the goddess Hestia. As the chief deity of the hearth, she oversaw not only fire used in the home but also the family and home life in general.

dim-witted Cronos, who had earlier betrayed and overthrown his own father, feared that Hestia and any other offspring of his might do the same to him. So he grabbed the new baby and swallowed her whole. Being divine, Hestia was immortal, so she remained alive in her father's gut.

Later, after Cronos had swallowed several more of his children, his last child, Zeus, escaped that fate and turned on the chief Titan. Cronos was forced to vomit up the swallowed deities, who by that time had grown to adulthood. Because she had been ingested first, Hestia was the last of the brood to be

Demeter and the Mysteries of Eleusis

Of the many Greek nature goddesses, one of the more important was Demeter, sister of Zeus, Hera, and Poseidon. The vital aspect of nature that Demeter oversaw included plants and agriculture. She was especially known as the chief protector and promoter of grains, which the Greeks viewed as crucial staffs of life. The breads and cereals made from wheat, barley, and other grains were essential in everyday Greek life, and it is not surprising that this goddess's main symbol was a sheaf of wheat.

No less importantly, Demeter was associated with one of the Greek world's most prominent religious shrines. The temple was erected as early as the 600s BCE at Eleusis, which lies about 12 miles (19.3 km) west of Athens's urban area. Demeter's temple was the focal point of the secretive Eleusinian Mysteries, religious ceremonies celebrated in her honor. The rites that took place within the shrine were known only to those who had undergone a special initiation. Modern experts have proposed that the rituals were somehow connected to a mystical cycle of life, death, resurrection, and immortality. Some evidence also suggests that the worshippers periodically reenacted the highlights of Demeter's chief myth. In it, Hades, lord of the underworld, kidnapped the goddess's daughter Persephone, whom Demeter diligently searched for over the course of many years. Eventually, a deal was struck whereby Persephone was allowed to be with her mother for half of each year but had to go back to Hades's shadowy realm during the other half.

disgorged. She then turned to her brother, Zeus, and asked him to grant her special status as a perpetually virgin goddess. A surviving Greek religious hymn states that she "swore a great oath which has in truth been fulfilled, that she would be a maiden [virgin] all her days. So Zeus the Father gave her a high honor instead of marriage, and she has her place [the hearth] in the midst of the house, and among all mortal men she is chief of the goddesses."[8]

Like the Gods Themselves

While Hestia was the first divinity the Greeks worshipped during the course of a given day, they often at least briefly saluted another female deity at the start of that day. She was Eos, goddess of the dawn, whom the Romans later called Aurora. Writers and artists typically described her as having rosy fingers or golden arms with which she opened some sort of sky gate. This made it possible for the sun god Helios to drive his blindingly bright chariot upward and across the heavens each day. One of the more vivid literary depictions of Eos was by the eighth-century-BCE epic poet Homer in his *Iliad*. "Eos in her saffron robe arose out of the ocean stream," he wrote, "bringing light for heaven and earth."[9]

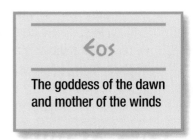

The goddess of the dawn and mother of the winds

In addition to that crucial service to nature, she was fruitful and gave birth to several other nature deities. With her first mate, the Titan Astraeus, she bore the wind gods Zephyrus, Boreas, and Notus and the deity who personified the morning star, Eosphoros. Eos also mated with a mortal named Tithonus, one of the sons of Troy's king Priam. It was from that union that her best-known myth comes. In that story, Eos was so enamored of the young and handsome Tithonus that she pleaded with Zeus to make him immortal like the gods themselves. The master of Olympus agreed to her request, but she forgot something of immense importance. She neglected to ask him to make sure Tithonus retained his youthful appearance and never grew older. As a result, over time the former Trojan prince continued to age yet could not die. In the words of the late, great modern myth teller Edith Hamilton:

> Helpless at last, unable to move hand or foot, he prayed for death but there was no release for him. He must live on forever, with old age forever pressing upon him more and more. At last in pity the goddess laid him in a room and left

him, shutting the door. There he babbled endlessly, words with no meaning. His mind had gone with his strength of body. He was only the dry husk of a man. There is a story too that he shrank and shrank in size until at last Eos, with a feeling for the natural fitness of things, turned him into the skinny and noisy grasshopper.[10]

The Mistress of Rainbows

Eos had a close connection with another female nature deity, Iris, goddess of the rainbow. Namely, Iris married Eos's son Zephyrus, the divine manifestation of the West Wind. In addition to manufacturing rainbows at appropriate moments, Iris had the no less important job of acting as the personal messenger for Zeus's wife, Hera, queen of the Olympian gods.

Although Iris played a small role in several Greek myths, her appearance in the tale of the great quest for the Golden Fleece is more pivotal. The hero Jason had assembled an impressive crew of brave warriors to help him track down the fleece—the skin of a magical ram—and deliver it to a Greek king. During the adventure-filled journey, these Argonauts (named for their vessel, the *Argo*), stopped on an island to gather food and water. There, they encountered Phineus, an old man who had irritated mighty Zeus.

As a punishment, Zeus had ordered the Harpies—hideous, smelly, flying creatures with sharp claws—to plague the old man. Each time Phineus sat down to eat, the Harpies, who happened to be siblings of the mistress of rainbows, Iris, would swoop down. They would either swipe the victim's food or squirt their putrid bodily fluids on it, rendering it inedible. Hence, the old man was constantly on the verge of starvation, a severe punishment indeed.

Taking pity on Phineus, Jason and the Argonauts decided to help him escape this plight. It happened that two of the *Argo*'s crew, Zetes and Calais, were sons of the North Wind deity, Boreas, which also made them Eos's grandsons. Like Eos and

An eighteenth-century painting depicts Eos, whom the Romans called Aurora, riding in her chariot. Sitting at right is her beloved Tithonus, who has by this time become quite elderly.

Boreas, the two warriors were able to fly. So the next time the Harpies appeared with the intent to interrupt old Phineus's meal, Zetes and Calais ambushed them. "Raising their swords," the ancient Greek myth teller Apollonius wrote, "the two sons of the North Wind flew off in pursuit."[11]

The airborne Argonauts managed to catch up to the vile creatures and were about to kill them when Iris caught sight of the gripping scene. In what seemed like an instant, she raced down from Mount Olympus and intervened. "Sons of Boreas," she shouted (according to Apollonius), "you may not touch the Harpies with your swords! They are the hounds of almighty Zeus. But I myself will undertake an oath that never again shall they come near to Phineus." Divine Iris subsequently proved true to her word. In Apollonius's epic poem, the *Argonautica*, he said, "This oath prevailed upon the noble brothers, who wheeled round and set their course for safety and the ship." Meanwhile, "the Harpies and Iris went their different ways. The Harpies withdrew to a den in Crete and Iris soared up to Olympus, cleaving the air with her unflagging wings."[12]

Nature's Numerous Nymphs

In overseeing fire, the dawn, and rainbows respectively, Hestia, Eos, and Iris represented only a tiny portion of the natural wonders the classical Greeks observed all around them. There were hundreds, and even thousands, of these, most of them minor in scope. Accordingly, Greek religious beliefs held, a separate deity must be in charge of each element of nature. In addition to a couple of dozen major or more familiar divine beings, therefore, it seemed logical that a great many minor ones must also exist.

For reasons that remain unclear, most of those minor nature deities were females. Collectively speaking, they were called nymphs, from the Greek word *nymphe*, meaning "a very attractive woman," especially a young bride. Indeed, all the nymphs were, or at least began as, beautiful young women. (A few were transformed into monsters by jealous goddesses.)

Most of these minor goddesses were seen to dwell within, and were more or less confined to, specific geographical natural places or environments. For example, there were nymphs who lived in rivers; others inhabited the oceans, lakes, streams, wells, islands, mountains, caves, trees, meadows, beaches, beehives, and even clouds. In addition, a few groups of nymphs were almost constant followers of specific deities—similar to groupies who hang around modern-day musicians. Dionysus, Artemis, Hermes, Poseidon, and Demeter, for instance, each had his or her personal swarm of loyal, adoring nymphs.

Demeter

The goddess of plants, agriculture, and grain crops

Yet despite their wide range of habitats and divine mentors, certain character traits were common among most nymphs. In particular, they tended to be very romantically inclined and both easily and quickly fell in love with humans and fellow divinities alike. Nymphs intensely displayed other human emotions as well,

The Famous Seven Sisters

Of the thousands of Greek minor goddesses known as nymphs, among the more familiar to people today are the Pleiades, seven sisters who can still be seen in a prominent star group in the night sky. The sisters were daughters of the Titan Atlas, who was himself famous for balancing earth's huge weight on his mighty shoulders and back. Their names were Electra, Maia, Taygete, Alcyone, Merope, Celaeno, and Sterope. Most of them produced notable children. For example, Electra gave birth to Dardanus, the founder of the Trojan race; Maia was the mother of the Olympian messenger god Hermes; and Alcyone bore the Greek king Hyreius.

In the Pleiades' principal myth, the giant hunter Orion fell in love with their mother, Pleione, and when she rejected his advances, he chased after her and her daughters. Although he could never quite catch up to them, he kept trying. Eventually, Zeus saw what was happening and took pity on the seven nymphs. He placed them, and Orion too, in the night sky, apparently to emphasize to future generations that the giant hunter would eternally trail behind them and they would always stay safe from his grasp. Over the centuries, farmers and others came to recognize that the rising of the sisters' little star group in the morning marks the beginning of summer.

sometimes including jealousy, unkindness, and severe cruelty. One of those mean-spirited nymphs was a river goddess named Nais. Retaliating against her boyfriend, Daphnis, who had cheated on her, she permanently blinded him.

In a similar vein, some nymphs earned reputations for being dangerous or even lethal. A case in point consisted of the famous Sirens, who appeared in several myths. Greek writers described them as seemingly beautiful women with lovely singing voices who lived on an uncharted island. When ships strayed too close to that perilous place, the Sirens would begin their enchanting songs, which the sailors could not resist. Those travelers invariably maneuvered their vessels to destruction on the jagged rocks lining the island's coasts.

In the story of Jason and the Argonauts, for example, the *Argo*'s gifted warrior-musician, Orpheus, heard the Sirens singing in the distance before anyone else on board noticed. He immediately pulled out his harp and started belting out his own melodies. His loud voice drowned out those of the Sirens as the ship sailed past the deadly island. (One crewman did hear the nymphs and dove into the water intending to go to them. But Aphrodite, goddess of love, saw what was happening and rescued him before he got very far.)

A nineteenth-century artist painted this colorful scene of the beautiful but deadly Sirens attempting to lure Odysseus and his crewmen to untimely deaths.

From the Talented to the Talkative

Fortunately for humanity, however, spiteful and dangerous nymphs were fairly rare. Most of these nature deities were friendly, kind, and harmless. Moreover, a few were talented at generating majestic natural phenomena. An example of the latter were the Hesperides, goddesses of the evening twilight and golden light of sunsets. Four in number, their names were Aegle, Erytheia, Hesperia, and Arethusa. The identity of their parents is uncertain, but the most accepted ancient tradition held that their father was the Titan Atlas, who was said to bear much of earth's bulk on his broad shoulders.

The Greeks also believed that magnificent golden sunsets could not happen without the Hesperides' influence. Somehow these sisters manufactured such displays, the story went. An unknown ancient writer described the evening nymphs "driving their two-horse chariot along the path of night to the new turning-point, where Nyx [goddess of night] passes through the light-bringing radiance in the eastern air."[13]

Although they are mentioned in a few myths, the Hesperides did not play major roles in those stories. One nymph who did have a prominent part in two fairly famous myths dwelled along the slopes of Mount Helicon, in the Greek mainland's central sector. Her name was Echo. Although she was extremely friendly and generous, she did possess one unfortunate character flaw, which was that she was overly talkative.

That trait got Echo into trouble one day while she was serving as an attendant to Zeus's wife, Hera. The latter was convinced that her husband was secretly seeing a mortal woman and decided to discover the truth by quietly spying on him. With Echo following along, Hera found a concealed spot in some bushes not far from a cottage that Zeus had entered shortly before. The stakeout went well, until suddenly Echo could no longer hold her silence and started chatting with the queen of Olympus. Even inside the cottage, Zeus clearly heard Echo's voice and deduced that Hera was lurking nearby. Furious with Echo for tipping off Zeus, Hera punished her by removing her ability to speak, *except* for repeating the last syllables of words people said to her. This, the Greeks believed, was the origin of the natural phenomenon named for the unfortunate nymph—the echo.

Even though she could no longer speak in a normal manner, Echo still had a tendency to fall in love with handsome men, as most nymphs did. The problem was that she now lavished her affections on a young man who loved only himself. Named Narcissus, he totally ignored poor Echo, who reacted by becoming depressed and no longer eating. Steadily, she grew increasingly thin until nothing was left of her but her voice, which, thanks to Hera, could only repeat the last things people said. Echo was gone. But the many other nature goddesses remained, and some people think they are still there today, ensuring that the natural environment continues to function normally.

Narcissus

A handsome, self-centered young man with whom the nymph Echo fell in love

---

Chapter Two

Mother Figures and Women's Protectors

The fact that Zeus, and not his divine wife, Hera, was the leader of the Olympian gods the ancient Greeks worshipped was no accident. Classical Greek society was patriarchal, and men occupied most of society's positions of power. It is not surprising, therefore, to see this male-dominated political and social structure reflected in their religious beliefs and practices, including the ladder of authority among the Greek gods.

Nevertheless, a fair amount of evidence suggests that this patriarchy did not always prevail among the inhabitants of the Greek geographical sphere. Before the Bronze Age Greek civilizations collapsed, giving way to the Dark Age, it appears that in Minoan society the primary deities were female. There was at least one mother goddess, or "Great Mother," who may have been called Potnia. (Some experts think this may have been a generic term referring to powerful goddesses as a whole.) This may well have reflected a partially matriarchal society among the Minoans themselves. If so, scholar Eva Cantarella explains, it was "a society characterized by a predominance of women within the family, in which marriage is matrilocal (the husband goes to the wife's house), descent is according to the female line, and rights of succession belong to the women, but in which the political power can be, and usually is, in the hands of the men."[14]

Cultural Connections: Zeus

Over the centuries, Hera's frequently unfaithful husband, Zeus, made an enormous impression on poets, painters, sculptors, musicians, and moviemakers. In the ancient world, dozens of temples honoring him were built across the Greek-speaking lands. Probably the most famous was the one at Olympia, site of the original Olympic Games. The giant statue of Zeus in that structure was listed as one of the Seven Wonders of the Ancient World. Later, during Europe's Renaissance (ca. 1300–ca. 1550), Zeus became the subject of great painters. In 1515, for instance, Italian artist Dosso Dossi produced a large canvas showing Zeus as an artist himself, painting butterflies. In 1811 another talented painter, France's Jean-Auguste-Dominique Ingres, created *Thetis Appeals to Zeus*, in which the sea nymph Thetis asks the god for a favor.

In the twentieth century, Zeus became a character in several expensive films having mythical themes. The great actor Laurence Olivier played him in the 1981 film *Clash of the Titans*, for instance. (Liam Neeson portrayed Zeus in the 2010 remake.) Perhaps the most outstanding screen version of the god was his portrayal by English actor Niall MacGinnis in *Jason and the Argonauts* (1963). Loaded with spectacular special effects, the film highly effectively shows Zeus, Hera, and the other Olympians as giants towering over the tiny human characters. In addition, a number of popular video games have featured Zeus, among them *Zeus: Master of Olympus*, by Vivendi Universal.

One theory holds that the Greek-speaking Mycenaeans, who lived on the Greek mainland, had a patriarchal social order, including among their deities. Increasing evidence supports the idea that the mainlanders invaded Minoan Crete around 1400 BCE. Subsequently, the matriarchal order of Potnia may have steadily given way to a patriarchal order that was eventually headed by Zeus.

Fast-forwarding to the classical Greek society that arose after the Dark Age, the Great Mother goddess concept, although no longer dominant, was by no means defunct. Very ancient cultural memories, probably kept alive through some of the Greek myths, emphasized that the earth itself harbored a divine intelligence in the form of the mother goddess Gaia. In addition, some of the Olympian goddesses, particularly Athena, Artemis, and Demeter, were said to possess at least traces of the old female-dominant Potnia dynamic. It occasionally surfaced momentarily at critical, emotional moments in their myths. Thus, even the patriarchal classical Greeks could not let go of a fascination for the notion of a powerful woman who can command the respect of men.

The Original Great Mother

In fact, throughout Greece's classical centuries, the earliest mother goddess in the Greek corpus of myths, Gaia, remained an integral player in the story of the cosmos's creation. After a long period in which random elements swirled aimlessly in a disordered mess called Chaos, two major regions of material existence—the earth and the sky—emerged. Moreover, these regions were not lifeless and mute like a rock. Instead, deep within their structures dwelled intelligent spirits capable of thought and reasoning. Gaia was the spirit residing within and personifying the earth's enormous bulk. Meanwhile, the vast sky that loomed above the earth was inhabited by her counterpart—Uranus, whom some Greeks called Father Heaven.

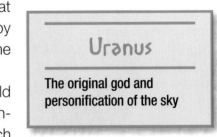

Uranus

The original god and personification of the sky

That these immense spirits would get to know each other was almost unavoidable, since they did live beside each other. No one knows why and how they went a step further and mated, but they did. The results—their offspring—were unlike any that the later humans and Olympian gods would produce. Some of Gaia's and Uranus's children were huge, malformed, and monstrous. The first three, for instance, each displayed fifty heads and a hundred hands, so the Greeks called them the *Hecatoncheires*, or "Hundred-handers." Gaia also gave birth to a number of one-eyed giants, the Cyclopes, and some other misshapen creatures.

Yet as time went on, the Great Mother concentrated hard on trying to beget more attractive offspring who were also very powerful. Finally, she succeeded and bore the initial members of the first race of gods, known to the Greeks as the Titans. In the words

Gaia was said to have mated with Tartarus, the underworld's deepest and scariest level. One of their offspring was the nightmarish creature Typhon, pictured in this artist's rendering.

of the seventh-century-BCE Greek poet Hesiod, "sending out unearthly music," later deities celebrated "the august race of firstborn gods, whom Earth [Gaia] bore to broad Heaven [Uranus], their progeny, givers of good things."[15]

Much later, well after the Olympian gods had defeated the Titans and taken charge of the cosmos, Gaia remained intact with at least some of her powers. Some ancient Greek writers held that she supplied Apollo, god of prophecy, with the special powers of perception he needed to run his famous oracle at Delphi. (The term *oracle* referred not only to his temple and sacred site, but also to the temple's priestess who served as a medium between him and human visitors.) Also, among the classical Greeks, reverence for the original Great Mother was so great that to swear something in Gaia's name was seen as the most binding of all oaths. Gaia even survived ancient Greece itself. In medieval and early modern times, people on the fringes of European society continued to believe in and pray to her.

Protector of Marriage and Home Life

The classical Greeks also recognized a different sort of mother goddess in Hera. In her case, she was the mother of the traditional pantheon of deities in the sense that she was the spouse of that group's father figure—Zeus. Perhaps in part because the two divinities were married, Hera early on emerged as the chief divine protector of marriage and women's home life. In that role, she could be expected to fight for the sanctity of marriage, including the concept of husbands being faithful to their wives. In this regard, Zeus certainly put his Olympian wife through her paces. Greek mythology is riddled with stories of his infidelity to her and her numerous fits of jealousy and attempts to punish his mistresses.

Hera was one of Zeus's sisters. Along with Hestia and their brothers Poseidon and Hades, they had been swallowed whole by their father, the leading Titan Cronos. Fortunately for all of these deities, Cronos had eventually vomited them up, allowing them to become part of a new race of gods—the Olympians.

The first time that Zeus viewed Hera in a romantic context occurred considerably later, after he had already had several mates and lovers (including the Titan Metis, mother of Athena, and Leto, who bore him Apollo and Artemis). One crisp winter day Zeus was strolling through a meadow and caught sight of Hera sunning herself beside a big boulder. As he often did, he decided to play the trickster and transform himself into a different form. In this case it was a cuckoo bird. Flying to her, he pretended to be freezing to death. Hera immediately felt her protective motherly side take over, and to keep the creature warm, she gently held it to her chest. This was the moment that Zeus chose to suddenly return to his true form, so the two were now locked in a close embrace.

Hera would have been content if her divine husband had continued to pay her the loving attention he did that day and for the year that followed. During that brief time she was happy in her role as queen of Mount Olympus and champion of home life among the mortal humans, whom she sincerely cared about. This explains the words of one of the surviving Greek hymns honoring her. "O royal Hera," it begins, "the race of mortals is your constant care." Moreover, "Mother of showers and winds, from you alone, producing all things, mortal home life is known. All [female] natures share your temperament divine, and universal sway alone is yours, with sounding blasts of wind, the swelling sea and rolling rivers roar when shook by you. Come, blessed goddess, famed almighty queen, [having a character] kind, rejoicing, and serene."[16]

Hera Versus Io and Semele

Hera's personality did not remain kind and serene for long, however. As happened so often with Zeus, he eventually grew bored with her and moved on to his next amorous conquest. Hoping to defend not only her own marriage but also the marriage institution in general, Hera often responded forcefully and sometimes

A nineteenth-century engraving shows Hera, disguised as an old woman, deceptively gaining the trust of Semele. Hera frequently and angrily sought vengeance against Zeus's mistresses.

even harshly. It was common for her to track down her errant husband's lovers and make them suffer in one way or another.

This was what happened in the case of Io, a princess of an early Greek kingdom, with whom Zeus had a torrid affair. Zeus realized that Hera was looking for Io, so he transformed the young woman into a cow. But Hera was not fooled. She convinced her husband to give her the cow as a present and then ordered one of her loyal followers, the many-eyed giant Argos, to keep an eye on the cow in case it tried to escape. In retaliation, Zeus told his divine messenger Hermes to kill Argos. This he did. However, Hera commanded Argos's ghost to harass Io, who, still in bovine form, wandered the earth in misery for many years. Zeus eventually got the upper hand when he finally changed Io back into a young woman.

It was Hera, however, who won the next round of the marital battles between Olympus's master and mistress. In the guise of a handsome young human man, Zeus struck up an intimate relationship with Semele, daughter of the founder of Thebes, Cadmus, and soon the princess was pregnant. Hera now employed one of her husband's own tricks by turning herself into an old woman. In that form, she gained Semele's trust and when the time was right urged her to demand that Zeus show her his true divine form.

Semele

A human princess whom Hera punished severely for sleeping with Zeus

---

"Make him prove his love," Hera suggested (according to the popular Roman myth teller Ovid). "Make him appear before you in the same fashion as when queen Hera takes him in her arms. Tell him to take you as he is in heaven, dressed in his glory!"[17]

Semele did as Hera (as the old woman) had advised. The princess convinced Zeus to display to her his true divine form, but it was so intensely radiant that her skin began to overheat and burn. The god suddenly considered that the fetus she was carrying would burn up as well, so he quickly reached into her womb and pulled the baby free. (The child grew up to be the fertility deity Dionysus.) Mere seconds later, Semele collapsed into a pile of ashes. Clearly, the young woman was no match— in either power or cunning—for the supreme Olympian wife and mother figure Hera.

The Phrygian Great Mother

Another mother goddess the Greeks highly venerated was not a member of the original Olympian pantheon. Over the course of the classical period and well beyond, the Greeks welcomed into their religion several goddesses who had originated in foreign lands. One of them was Cybele, a deity initially worshipped in Phrygia, a region of west-central Anatolia (now Turkey). That the Greeks would be exposed to her was almost inevitable. This was because the western coastal area of Anatolia, bordering the Aegean

Isis: The Model Mother

Cybele was not the only mother goddess the Greeks adopted from a foreign people. They also borrowed Isis from the Egyptians. In one sense, Isis was a fertility deity who made sure that humans had enough productive soil in which to grow their food. She also resembled Hera, in that she protected the marriage institution (although she lacked Hera's constant suspicions and jealousies of her husband). In addition, Isis was a model mother figure who carefully nurtured her loving son, Horus, whom the Greeks called Harpocrates.

Both Egyptian and Greek artists often portrayed Isis holding or nursing her young son, a visual image that influenced later Christian depictions of the Virgin Mary holding her own son, Jesus. In the most important myth about Isis that transferred from Egyptian to Greek culture, she was deeply in love with her husband, Osiris, king of Egypt. Osiris's brother, the jealous and wicked Seth, murdered the king, chopped up his body into thousands of pieces, and scattered them throughout the known world. The loving, courageous, and resourceful Isis refused to let this crime stand. Although it took her many years, she tracked down all of Osiris's body parts, pieced them back together, and used magical spells to reanimate his body. As was true elsewhere in the Mediterranean world, worship of Isis in the Greek lands included a special initiation into her cult, including baptism and the promise of eternal salvation, customs that also influenced the earliest Christians.

Sea on one side and Phrygia on the other, was long a prosperous Greek cultural sphere. During the fifth century BCE, merchants and other travelers brought knowledge of Cybele, nicknamed the "Great Mother," into the Greek lands. By the middle of the following century, regular worship of her in those lands had become fairly common.

Cybele was essentially a fertility deity who guaranteed that the soil of farmlands would remain rich and produce many good har-

An engraving dating to the 1840s shows Cybele, originally an Anatolian goddess, flanked by lions, which for the Greeks symbolized her status as mistress of animals and the natural world.

vests. But another side of her personality was that of a life-giving nature-based mother, in some ways similar to Gaia. In that capacity, worshippers believed that Cybele could cure disease. So people sometimes brought sick relatives or friends to her shrines in hopes that she would make them well. A third side of her character pictured her as a protective mother who might shield worshippers during wartime.

One way that the Greeks made Cybele's transition into their religion as smooth as possible was to put their own spin on an old Phrygian myth. Supposedly, the goddess was created by a very ancient male deity worshipped throughout Phrygia. The Greeks decided that that male god was none other than Zeus. In Cybele's Greek birth myth, therefore, one day Zeus was napping in a meadow on a mountainside and a bit of his sperm leaked and fell to the ground. Within a short time, a magnificent being sprang up from that sacred spot. At first, it had both female and male sex organs. But soon it shed the male organ, and then, being fully female, she assumed the persona of Cybele. Her discarded male part was not wasted, however, since it later produced a handsome young man named Attis, whom Cybele dearly loved. Greeks who attended her shrines often frequently honored Attis as part of their worship of her.

A Humanitarian Mind-Set

Just as Attis was closely associated with Cybele, other mother goddesses enjoyed the assistance of lesser but still important deities. One of the oldest and most popular of these supernatural helpers was Eileithyia. Said to be Hera's daughter by Zeus and Hera's chief female associate, she was widely viewed as the deity of childbirth and labor pains.

In Greek, Eileithyia's name literally means "she who comes to relieve." Clearly, this referred to her relieving some of

> **Eileithyia**
>
> Hera's daughter and the goddess of childbirth and labor pains

the physical pains connected to having a baby. Homer mentioned her performance of that service in his *Iliad*, saying, "As the sharp sorrow of pain descends on a woman in labor, the bitterness that the hard spirits of childbirth bring on" can be lessened by Hera's daughter, "who holds the power of the bitter birth-pangs."[18]

In Eileithyia's best-known myth, she helped with the birth of the famous strongman and hero Heracles (today better known as Hercules). Initially, she did not expect to help at all. This was because Hera was furious with the mother, Alcmena, for sleeping with Zeus and ordered Eileithyia to use a dark magical charm to foul up the birth process. That way, Hera hoped, both the mother and child might die. To that end, Eileithyia sat outside Alcmena's room for days with her arms, legs, fingers, and toes crossed—postures intended to initiate the hurtful charm. Suddenly, however, one of the midwives screamed loudly. Distracted, Eileithyia uncrossed her limbs, eradicating the charm and throwing her into her usual humanitarian mind-set. Leaping into action, she made sure that Heracles was born healthy.

Heracles

Also known as Hercules, the famous Greek hero renowned for his superhuman strength and big heart

When divine female protectors such as Cybele, Hera, and Eileithyia performed their normal divine duties, they won the praise of male Greek leaders, thinkers, and writers. The poet Pindar extolled the virtues of Eileithyia, for example, saying, "Without you, we see not the day or the black night!" Thanks to her efforts as "bringer of children to birth," he added, "do we all draw breath!"[19] Without such caring goddesses, he seemed to say, people could not even exist, much less prosper.

Chapter Three

Lovers and Patrons of the Arts

Several of the Greek goddesses were known as supremely beautiful women, passionate lovers, and steadfast supporters of the arts. For the classical Greeks, there was a solid connection between love and beauty, and between beauty and great art. In part this was because the deities who oversaw love and beauty were invariably beautiful themselves. Also, it was thought that some of these goddesses actually specialized in inspiring artists to create beautiful works.

Most of all, love, beauty, and art were forever linked through the miracle of the Athenian golden age, the burst of artistic brilliance that took place in Athens during the fifth and fourth centuries BCE. Never before or since did so many great artists of all kinds come together in one place and together produce such a singular expression of national genius. As the late scholar Thomas Craven stated it, Athenian sculptors and painters strove mightily and lovingly to depict both divine and human figures as faithfully as possible. In the process, Craven explained, they created figures "beyond those produced by nature." Among them were "marbles which reveal living flesh within the polished surfaces, faces of god-like serenity, women in costumes of infinite grace" and "figures of indescribable nobility."[20]

Birth of the Love Goddess

Of the majestic artistic works created in Athens and other Greek city-states during that remarkable age, a great many were based on the characters and events of the Greek myths. Particularly popular in public places were statues and paintings of the loveliest goddesses. Carved and painted figures of Athena, Artemis, Hera, and other female divinities adorned temples, shrines, and town squares all over the Greek-speaking world.

Especially beloved as a model by artists was Aphrodite, goddess of love, beauty, and pleasure. Painters and sculptors always pictured her as a beautiful woman, either partially clothed or more often nude. Frequently, her son, the winged love god Eros (the Roman Cupid) was depicted beside her, although she was always the center of attention.

Eros

The handsome son of Aphrodite, he had the power to make one person fall in love with another

One of the best-known of Aphrodite's many myths is the one in which she was born and first met the other Olympian deities. According to Hesiod in his epic poem, the *Theogony*, she arose from the sea under some decidedly unusual conditions. When the Titan Cronos attacked his father, Uranus, the latter's genitals were sliced off and fell into the water. The impact created a large amount of foam, which spiraled round and round and seemed to pulsate with a life of its own. Both people and gods gathered from all around to see this strange phenomenon.

After many hours, everyone gasped. Rising up from the still-spinning sea foam was a breathtakingly beautiful female figure— the divine Aphrodite. All the female deities present were immediately impressed and moved to help her onto the dry land. One of her ancient hymns tells how those goddesses joyously

clothed her with heavenly garments. On her head they put a fine, well-wrought crown of gold, and in her pierced ears they hung ornaments of yellow metal and precious gold, and adorned her with golden necklaces over her soft neck and snow-white breasts. [And] when they had fully decked her, they brought her to the [leading male] gods, who [were] amazed at [her] beauty.[21]

The Judgment of Paris

Of the many male deities who vied for Aphrodite's hand, the lucky one, at least at first, was the divine smith of Mount Olympus's enormous forge, Hephaestus. What he did not realize was that, despite her good looks, she was fickle when it came to the opposite sex. Behind his back she began to dally with Ares, god of war. When Hephaestus found out about the goddess's infidelity, he alerted the other deities, most of whom scolded Aphrodite and Ares.

Aphrodite was not only fickle but also quite vain about her beauty. Because of that conceit, she helped set in motion the

In 1485 Renaissance artist Sandro Botticelli painted this widely famous image of Aphrodite's birth from a mass of sea foam as other divine beings look on in wonder.

most famous of the larger-scale Greek mythological events—the Trojan War. It all began with a seemingly harmless contest to decide which of three goddesses—Hera, Aphrodite, and Athena—was the most beautiful. The three urged Zeus to judge the competition. But not wanting to deal with the ire of the two losers, he wisely declined. Instead, he suggested, they could seek out Paris, a handsome prince of the powerful city of Troy, since he was said to be an outstanding judge of beauty.

The three contenders took Zeus's advice, found Paris, and persuaded the youth to judge their contest. Each goddess tried

Cultural Connections: Homer's Epics

Aphrodite, who plays a key role in Homer's epic of the Trojan War, the *Iliad*, is only one of several goddesses who appear in that work, as well as in Homer's other great epic, the *Odyssey*, about the Greek king Odysseus's wanderings after that conflict. The other goddesses depicted in those epics include the Muses, Themis, Hera, Iris, Athena, and Artemis. Thus, for the classical Greeks these works were in a sense treasure chests of information about those deities. This is one of the reasons that Homer's epics penetrated and remained ever popular in Western culture over the centuries, touching all aspects of the arts and literature. During the European Renaissance, for instance, dozens of paintings and sculptures depicted characters and events from the two epics. Later, numerous literary works based on them also appeared, including William Shakespeare's play *Troilus and Cressida* (1602) and Edgar Allan Poe's poem "To Helen" (1831), in which he famously quipped that her face had launched a thousand ships. Later still, in the twentieth century, the Irish writer James Joyce based his classic novel *Ulysses* on the *Odyssey*. (Ulysses was the Roman name for Odysseus.) In that same century, numerous movies about the Trojan War and Odysseus's adventures were made. These include *Ulysses* (1954), with Kirk Douglas in the title role; *Helen of Troy* (1956); *The Trojan Women* (1971); *The Odyssey* (1997), with Armand Assante as Odysseus; and *Troy* (2004), with Brad Pitt as Achilles and Orlando Bloom as Paris.

to bribe him into choosing her, and Aphrodite offered him something he could not easily resist. If he chose her as the winner, she said, she would make the most beautiful woman in the world fall in love with him. This did indeed sway the young man. In what became known as the Judgment of Paris, he proclaimed Aphrodite the winner of the contest.

It so happened that the most beautiful living mortal woman at that moment was Helen, wife of the king of the Greek kingdom of Sparta. When Paris soon visited that realm, Aphrodite kept her word and made Helen fall for him. The young lovers ran off to Troy together. Helen's husband then called on other Greek kings to help him get her back, and a mighty Greek expedition laid siege to Troy for ten years. Throughout that conflict, Aphrodite supported the Trojans and was sorely disappointed when they lost.

Divine Overseer of Chance and Luck

Troy's bad fortune was decided by a force that the Greeks believed was even more powerful than Zeus and his Olympian brethren. That force was fate. Even the gods, the popular wisdom held, could not change one of its major predictions, one of which was that a Greek army would one day destroy Troy.

Nevertheless, there were countless thousands of possible outcomes for smaller-scale happenings, with which fate did not waste its time. In such cases, Tyche, goddess of chance and good or bad luck, often (though not always) had a hand. *Tyche* was a commonly used shortened form of her full name— Eutychia. By custom, people used the longer version mainly when she brought success, prosperity, and especially long-lasting feelings of love. Whatever one might call her, Greek artists depicted her as a beautiful female human men could long for and human women could envy.

Tyche

The goddess of fortune, chance, and good or bad luck

Regardless of their gender, all Greeks believed that Tyche could potentially affect their lives in either positive or negative ways, especially in matters of love and happiness. So people tended fairly often to offer her prayers or to praise her, hoping to stay on her good side. A surviving short prayer to her states, "Tyche, beginning and end for mankind, you sit in wisdom's seat and give honor to mortal deeds. From you comes more good than evil, grace shines about your gold wing, [you] see a way out of the impasse in troubles, and you bring bright light in darkness, you most excellent of goddesses."[22]

In one of her myths, originally told by the noted seventh-century-BCE Greek storyteller Aesop, Tyche noticed a traveler who was extremely tired from walking all day. The man laid down beside a deep well, drifted off, and was about to fall in when the goddess swiftly intervened. After awakening him, she said, "Good Sir, pray wake up. For if you fall into the well, the blame will be thrown on me, and I shall get an ill name among mortals. For I find that men are sure to impute their calamities to me, however much by their own folly they have really brought them on themselves."[23] From this story, it appears that Tyche was quite concerned with how mortals viewed her. In fact, having many humanlike emotions, all the Greek goddesses tended to fret about their images, and at times each worried that mortals might be neglecting her in favor of other female deities. That even Tyche harbored such worries is revealed in another of her myths. In it she heard about a farmer who had accidentally discovered a cache of valuable gold while plowing his field. Excited over this find, the man erected an altar on his land and used it to give thanks by worshipping the earth goddess Gaia, who he assumed had made the discovery possible. This upset Tyche, who felt that she should have been the focus of the worship. She appeared to him and delivered him a warning. If someone ever stole his gold, she said, and he prayed to her for aid, she would remember his slight to her and refuse to help.

Encouraging Life's Best Qualities

Although Tyche might and often did bring love and happiness to selected humans, three other goddesses dedicated all their efforts to bringing happiness to people and deities alike. Known as the Graces, they pursued that noble goal by their very natures, which were kind, loving, and generous. The Graces regularly promoted what most Greeks viewed as life's best qualities. These included elegance, attractiveness, joy, festivity, laughter, dancing, singing, play, feasts, lovemaking, and relaxation.

As they encouraged life's pleasures, the Graces were often invited to accompany other deities. In ancient Greek art, for example, both Hera and Aphrodite can frequently be seen walking or lounging with one or more of the Graces. Artists typically portrayed the Graces themselves as beautiful young women wearing little or no clothing, holding hands with one another, and wearing myrtle sprigs in their hair.

In another of Botticelli's renowned works—the Primavera *(1487)—a group of deities celebrate the coming of springtime. They include the three Graces, who join hands and dance at left.*

The classical Greeks, as Edith Hamilton memorably said, "were in love with play and played magnificently." Indeed, "to rejoice in life, and to find the world beautiful and delightful to live in, was a mark of the Greek spirit."[24] It is not surprising, therefore, that the Greeks held the Graces in high esteem and addressed them in both prayers and songs. Pindar composed this prayer to the three elegant goddesses: "Queens of song, [you] Graces who watch over [humankind], hear when I pray. By your help, all sweet and delightful things belong to men. If anyone is wise or lovely or famous [you had a hand in it]. For without the aid of the holy Graces, not even the gods [can properly stage] dances or feasts. The Graces [help with] all that is done in heaven."[25]

Graces

Three female deities who promoted beauty, joy, festivities, and other good qualities of life

---

The Graces also watched over celebrations of victories, especially those involving winning athletes in the many sporting competitions held across the Greek lands each year. In his *Ninth Olympian Ode*, Pindar recounted how the Graces regularly helped spread the glorious news that an athlete from a certain Greek city had won an Olympic event. Putting words into the mouth of one of the Graces, he wrote, "On that dear city I kindle light with flaming songs, and faster than thoroughbred horse or ship on the wing, I shall send this news to every quarter."[26]

The Stirring Sounds of the Muses

While the Graces supported the overall enjoyment of life, they lacked the power to inspire individual humans with the talent and ideas needed to create the many kinds of artistic works that Greek civilization produced. That special power belonged to a second set of benevolent goddesses known as the Muses. Perhaps the most famous ancient reference to these delightful deities was the one uttered by Hesiod in the opening of his *Theogony*. In that long poem, he sought to describe in stirring words the creation of the gods and appealed to the Muses for whatever inspiration they might throw his way. "Hail, daughters of Zeus!" he began. "Give me sweet song, to celebrate the holy race of gods who live forever, sons of starry Heaven and Earth, and gloomy Night, and salty Sea. Tell how the gods and earth arose at first, and rivers

An Unwise Challenge to the Muses

In one of the more famous myths about the Muses, the Greek king Pierus had nine daughters and named them after those renowned female deities. As the girls grew up, they came to believe that they were just as skilled as the Muses. So Pierus challenged the nine goddesses to a contest with his daughters. Several hundred nymphs agreed to judge the competition, which did not go well for the princesses. Through the supposed recollection of one of the Muses, the popular Roman poet Ovid told what happened:

> The nymphs agreed unanimously that the [Muses] were the victors. Our defeated opponents replied by hurling abuses at us, until I exclaimed, "So, it is not enough that you have deserved punishment by forcing this contest, but you add insult to injury? Our patience is not unlimited. We shall [now] proceed to punish you." The [young] women laughed and scorned my threats, but as they tried to speak, menacing us with loud cries and wanton gestures, they saw feathers sprouting from their nails and plumage covering their arms. They looked at each other, watching their faces narrow into horny beaks, as a new addition was made to the birds of the forest. When they tried to beat their breasts, the movement of their arms raised them, to hover in the air. They had become magpies, the scandal-mongers of the woods. Even now, as birds, they will retain their original power of speech. They will chatter harshly and have an insatiable desire to talk.

Ovid, *Metamorphoses*, trans. Mary M. Innes. London: Penguin, 2006, p. 133.

and the boundless swollen sea and shining stars, and the broad heaven above. [Tell] me these things, Olympian Muses, tell from the beginning!"[27]

Although a few ancient writers placed the number of Muses at three, most agreed with Hesiod that there were nine. Most also accepted the names and specialties he listed for them. Melpomene oversaw tragic drama, he said, and Thalia comedic drama. In addition, Calliope inspired epic poetry; Terpsichore, lyric poetry and dance; Erato, lyric poetry and songs; Clio, history;

Artist Charles Meynier created this 1800 painting of Erato, the muse of love poetry. At the start of the third book of his Argonautica, *the Greek writer Apollonius asked Erato to inspire his writing.*

Euterpe, flute playing; Polymnia, mime; and Urania, astronomy. Hesiod also indicated that these goddesses sometimes worked under the direction of the Olympian god of prophecy and the arts, Apollo.

All the gods and goddesses appreciated the Muses, as revealed in an early hymn recited by human worshippers. Divine Apollo journeyed from earth to Olympus, the hymn begins, "to join the gathering of the other gods. Then straightway the undying gods think only of the lyre [harp] and song, and all the Muses together, voice sweetly answering voice, hymn the unending gifts the gods enjoy."[28]

On a more somber note, the Muses also sometimes attended the funerals of fallen human heroes and sang dirges, or songs of grief, so moving that it was said that even the most hardened warriors wept. The most famous funeral the Muses attended was that of the great Greek warrior Achilles, the central character of Homer's epic of the Trojan War, the *Iliad*. As told by King Odysseus in Homer's

Achilles

The formidable Greek warrior who fought and died at Troy

other epic, the *Odyssey*, the nine Muses surrounded Achilles's corpse, "chanting your dirge [sweetly] till not a dry eye was to be seen in all the Greek force, so poignant [touching] was the Muses' song."[29]

Every Greek totally understood the Muses' role in this sad scene. For the Greeks, there was no contradiction between the joys of creation and the creative expression of grief. In Hamilton's words, they were "terribly aware of life's uncertainty and the imminence of death. Over and over again they emphasize the brevity and failure of all human endeavor, the swift passing of all that is beautiful and joyful,"[30] and the Muses helped them endure that awful but inevitable transition.

Chapter Four

Those Who Deal in Prophecy and Sorcery

Magic was an ever-prevalent and troubling concept in ancient Greece. The Greeks recognized a clear difference between religious rituals, in which people asked the gods for favors, and magical rituals, in which a person tried to make something supernatural happen on his or her own. Well-educated Greeks usually dismissed magic as nonsense. Many ordinary Greeks, however, were superstitious and believed that certain kinds of magic might be effective. The rituals usually involved handling animal parts in a set manner, casting a spell using someone's hair or nail clippings, repeatedly chanting certain strange phrases, or wearing special jewelry said to ward off evil. Considering such beliefs, it is not surprising that stories about goddesses who practiced sorcery crept into the Greek corpus of myths.

Meanwhile, prophecy—the prediction of future events—was generally accepted as a real phenomenon by virtually all Greeks. One of the chief concepts of both religion and mythology was the oracle, a message that a priestess supposedly relayed from a god to humans. The priestess herself was also called an oracle, as was the sacred site where she delivered the message.

At Greece's most famous oracle—Apollo's temple at Delphi (in central Greece)—religious pilgrims asked the priestess questions. Her assistants, typically men, stood near her and translated the generally inarticulate sounds making up her answers. The translations themselves tended to be obscure and open to varying interpretation. So political, social, and religious leaders often argued about what the delivered messages meant and how people should react to them. Like sorcery, the mysterious, supernatural qualities surrounding oracles inevitably made their way into the Greek myths, in which several female deities were said to be oracles or prophetesses.

The First Delphic Oracle

One of the more powerful of those goddesses was Themis, a member of the original race of gods—the Titans. Versatile for a single deity, she was seen as overseer of natural law and divine justice, as well as a prophetess of future events. On the basis of these qualities, Greek artists pictured her holding a sword, with which she supposedly could separate fact from fiction. Over time, such artistic depictions made her the early prototype of Lady Justice, a popular character in Western civilization right up to the present. (The blindfold she wears in modern versions was added in later centuries and did not originate with the Greeks.)

Themis's potent ability to predict the future allowed her to become the first of the Delphic oracles. In fact, one of her main myths recounts how the earth goddess Gaia originally oversaw the sacred grounds at Delphi and passed their control to Themis. There the Titan erected the first of a succession of temples that graced the site, became the first oracle, and eventually gave the place to Apollo.

A myth in which Themis plays a small but critical role centers on her famous son, the Titan Prometheus. In the

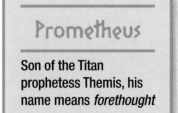

Prometheus

Son of the Titan prophetess Themis, his name means *forethought*

original tale, dramatized by the Athenian playwright Aeschylus in *Prometheus Bound* (written ca. 460 BCE), Themis passed her gift of prophecy on to her son. With this ability, he was able

An early modern painting depicts the oracle of Apollo's temple at Delphi delivering a prophecy to some religious pilgrims. Such prophecies were open to interpretation.

to foretell that Zeus and the Olympians would defeat the Titans. Hence, in order for Prometheus to secure a decent future, it made sense for him to switch sides and help Zeus.

This is revealed in Aeschylus's play when Prometheus lies chained to a rock—a punishment ordered by Zeus in retaliation for Prometheus giving humans fire. A visitor approaches, and Prometheus tells him how he inherited the gift of foresight from Themis. As a result, "I knew the appointed course of things to come," the chained god says. "My mother, Themis, [had] many times foretold to me that not brute strength, not violence, but cunning must give victory to the rulers of the future."[31]

The Tragedy of Oenone

Another goddess who possessed the gift of prophecy, Oenone, was a mountain nymph who inhabited the slopes of Mount Ida, not far from Troy. One ancient account claimed that she learned how to foretell certain future events from Zeus's mother, the Titan Rhea. (It was said that Gaia also had that ability and passed it on to her daughter Rhea.)

Oenone met Paris, son of Troy's King Priam, when the young man was a shepherd working in Ida's lush meadows, and the nymph and prince fell in love. Because she could see at least some future events, Oenone urged Paris to remain always with her on Ida's slopes. Her foresight told her that if he left and traveled across the Aegean to Greece, awful things would happen. Thus, when Aphrodite caused Paris to fall in love

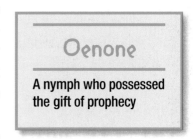

Oenone

A nymph who possessed the gift of prophecy

with Sparta's queen, Helen, and he sailed away to find her, Oenone was beside herself with worry. The nymph now foresaw an enormous war that would be fought between the Trojans and Greeks, a conflict in which Paris would die.

During the ten-year-long Greek siege of Troy, Oenone allowed bitterness over Paris's abandonment of her to rule her life, and she made no effort to reconcile with him. During the final year of the war, however, the Greek archer Philoctetes badly wounded Paris, and some Trojans sent for Oenone, hoping she might help heal him. Still angry, she initially refused. But soon she had a change of heart and rushed to Troy to see him. The great tragedy of her life was that she arrived just after his death, and she never had the chance to forgive him and bid him farewell. In a cruel twist of fate, her prophetic abilities had never revealed to her this sad scenario. According to the fourth-century-CE Greek epic poet Quintus Smyrnaeus, she cried out, "Woe for my wickedness! O hateful life! I loved my hapless husband, dreamed with him [and desired to remain] hand in hand, and heart in heart! The gods ordained not so. Oh had the black Death-Demons snatched me from the earth before I from Paris turned away in hate! My living love has left me! Yet will I dare to die with him!"[32] Seconds later, totally overcome with grief, she took her own life.

Aeaea's Resident Sorceress

The Greeks drew a distinct line between goddesses like Oenone, who never used their special gifts to hurt anyone, and divine sorceresses who often used their powers in unethical ways. The beautiful but dangerous witch Circe was a well-known example. Said to be a daughter of Helios, god of the sun, she dwelled on a remote island called Aeaea, where merchants and other travelers occasionally landed to find food and water. Some of them never made it off the island because Circe felt they had offended her in some way, and as a punishment she turned them into wolves, lions, pigs, and other animals.

Of the wanderers who landed on Aeaea and encountered its resident sorceress, the most famous was the Greek hero Odysseus. He and his surviving followers, among them his old friend Macareus, had endured several hardships after departing Troy and subsequently losing their way in uncharted seas. Odysseus ordered Macareus to take some men and make contact with whoever might live on the island.

Later, Macareus told how, when he reached Circe's house, she welcomed him and his men with refreshments. Unknown to them, he said, she had cast a spell on them, causing them to turn into pigs. He recalled (according to Ovid's telling of the myth):

> We took from the goddess's hand the cups she gave us and drained them greedily, for we were parched. As soon as we had done so, the dread goddess touched our hair lightly with her wand, and [soon] my body began to bristle with stiff hairs, and I was no longer able to speak, but uttered harsh grunts instead of words. My body bent forward and down, until my face looked straight at the ground, and I felt my mouth hardening into a turned-up snout.[33]

Eventually, the god Hermes intervened. With his help, Odysseus and Circe worked out a sort of truce and developed some

Artist John William Waterhouse's 1891 painting shows the sorceress Circe offering Odysseus a drink. Fortunately for him, he refused, which kept him from being transformed into a pig.

mutual trust, and she agreed to change Macareus and the other Greeks back into human form. Furthermore, when Odysseus decided it was time to depart the island, she gave him some valuable advice. He must travel to a little-known hole in the earth that leads to a portion of the underworld. There, she explained,

A Sorceress Asks Nyx for Help

One Greek goddess, Nyx, was not seen specifically as a sorceress or witch herself. Yet because she was often associated with death and dark and mysterious places, some villains in mythology called on her to use her divine powers to help them commit evil deeds. According to Hesiod, Nyx was an extremely ancient being who emerged from chaos in the cosmos's infancy and personified the dark night. Greek artists usually depicted her as either flying via a pair of wings or riding in a chariot. Part of her importance in mythology was based on her giving birth to a number of deities connected to life's darker realties, including Thanatos, god of death; Eris, goddess of strife; and Oizys, goddess of misery and pain. One example of a human requesting that Nyx help her cast a dark, hurtful spell occurs in the myths of the sorceress Medea. According to Ovid, Medea

> stole out of her home, dressed in flowing robes, with her feet bare, her head uncovered, and her hair streaming over her shoulders. [Only] the stars, unresting, sparkled in the sky. Stretching up her arms to these stars, Medea turned herself about three times, [and] three times uttered a wailing cry. Then, sinking to her knees on the hard earth, [she called out] "O Nyx, most faithful guardian of my secrets, [be with me now]. By your help, I can [make] mountains tremble [and] ghosts rise from their tombs!"

Ovid, *Metamorphoses*, trans. Mary M. Innes. London: Penguin, 2006, p. 160.

he would find Tiresias, "the blind Theban prophet, whose understanding even death has not impaired. [He] has a mind to reason with," whereas the other ghosts surrounding him "are mere shadows flitting to and fro." Only Tiresias could help Odysseus and his men find their home, "and he will lay down for you your journey [and] direct you home across the fish-delighting seas."[34]

Surrounded by an Air of Mystery

Despite her reputation as an untrustworthy witch, Circe had come to admire Odysseus, and as a result she proved true to her word. He followed her instructions and did find Tiresias's ghost, who proved helpful to the roving Greeks. That she knew so much about the ghosts of the dead and where to find an entrance to their gloomy realm was not surprising. Deities who practiced dark sorcery always knew of such murky and disquieting things.

Indeed, the same could be said for a mysterious fertility goddess whom the Greeks associated with fear of the unknown, death, ghosts, demons, and black magic. Her name was Hecate. Several different accounts of her origins circulated in the ancient world, the most commonly accepted being that of Hesiod. He claimed she was a Titan whom Zeus respected so much that he allowed her to keep her powers after the Olympians' victory over the first race of gods.

Befitting the vague mystical attributes often associated with Hecate, some of the details of her worship are unclear. More certain is that the Greeks and many other ancients saw crossroads as having magical properties. Evidence shows that on the last day of each month, Hecate's worshippers placed small food offerings to her at crossroads. In art, the Greeks frequently showed her as having three faces and holding a torch, perhaps to light her way when she visited the shadowy land of the dead.

Hecate was also often associated with plants, especially poisonous ones. Coupled with the air of mystery surrounding her, some legends depicted human sorcerers and witches asking her to help poison their enemies. In the myth of Jason and the Argonauts, for example, it is established that Hecate taught the human witch Medea how to use drugs as poisons and to weave magical spells. Later, after Jason brought Medea to Greece and betrayed her, she sought revenge and called on Hecate. There is no other deity she venerates more, Medea

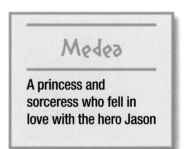

Medea

A princess and sorceress who fell in love with the hero Jason

This 1907 painting shows Medea mixing a magic potion for Jason, who looks on. With her aid, Jason was able to steal the fabulous Golden Fleece from her father, King Aeëtes.

states in Euripides's great play *Medea*. She is "my chosen accomplice," the woman says, "to whose presence my central hearth is dedicated. No one shall hurt me and not suffer for it!"[35]

A Twisted Series of Events

Not long after uttering those defiant words, Medea herself proceeded to do the hurting. She killed the children she had had with Jason as a way of punishing him. In the Greek myths, each sorceress—whether human like Medea or divine like Circe—had one major cruel or unkind act for which she became best known ever after. For Medea it was child murder, and for Circe it was transforming humans into animals.

For Circe's sister Pasiphae, another daughter of the sun god and another skilled practitioner of black magic, the act that ended up defining her for the ages was bestiality, having sexual relations with an animal. The story of how Pasiphae stooped to that level began years before with her marriage to Minos, king of Crete. She bore him several children and at first was happy.

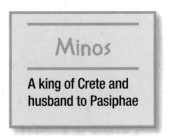

Minos

A king of Crete and husband to Pasiphae

But as time went on, the Cretan queen learned that her husband was frequently cheating on her. Angry, she decided to retaliate through the use of her magic. This consisted of spells she cast that made scorpions and other poisonous creatures zero in on and kill Minos's mistresses.

Although Pasiphae managed to achieve vengeance on her husband without physically harming him, she later came to regret sparing his life. Behind her back, Minos attempted to solidify his power on the throne by making a deal with the god of the seas, Poseidon. If that deity would conjure up a magnificent bull, the king would sacrifice it to the sea god, whose ego would thereby be hugely stroked. Poseidon kept his end of the bargain by producing the bull. But Minos cheated by secretly keeping the animal for himself and sacrificing an ordinary bull instead.

Poseidon was not fooled, however, and proceeded to punish Minos by making his queen debase both herself and the royal marriage. According to the second-century-CE Greek writer known as Pseudo-Apollodorus, the god caused Pasiphae to "develop a lust for the bull. In her passion for it, she took on as her accomplice [the royal architect], Daedalus, [who] built a wooden cow on wheels, skinned a real cow, and sewed the contraption into the skin, and then, after placing Pasiphae inside, set it in a meadow where the bull normally grazed."[36]

A twisted series of events then transpired. Thinking the artificial cow was real, the bull mated with it. But because Pasiphae was inside the device, she was the one impregnated by the beast. Several months later, she gave birth to a child she called Asterios, but nearly everyone else labeled the child Minotaur, or "Minos

The Cretan Bulls: The Truth Behind the Myths?

In a famous myth, Crete's King Minos acquires a powerful bull from Poseidon. Soon afterward, Minos's wife, Pasiphae, mates with the creature. She then gives birth to the monstrous Minotaur—which is part man and part bull. This is only one of many ancient tales and references to the cultural importance of bulls in ancient Crete. Archaeological evidence shows that Crete's Bronze Age Minoan civilization either worshipped bulls or used them in their worship. Also, surviving wall paintings indicate that large-scale athletic games involving bulls were prominent in Minoan Crete.

Given these facts, historians have considered how the myth of Pasiphae and the Minotaur might bear grains of truth. About the renowned bull-man, the first-century-BCE Greek historian Diodorus Siculus wrote, "This creature, they say, was of double form, the upper parts of the body as far as the shoulders being those of a bull and the remaining parts those of a man." Some evidence suggests that in some Minoan religious ceremonies, priests wore bull masks, an image that over time might easily have been misinterpreted as a half-bull monster. Also, some experts surmise, in another ritual a priestess may have acted out a symbolic "marriage" of a human woman and a bull, with a priest in a bull mask playing the role of the bull. Distorted by centuries of misunderstanding and exaggeration, such images from Minoan religion might well have given rise to Pasiphae's disturbing story.

Diodorus Siculus, *Library of History*, vol. 3, trans. Charles H. Oldfather. Cambridge, MA: Harvard University Press, 1954, p. 61.

bull." It had the head and face of a bull and the body of a human, and because it was wild and bloodthirsty, Minos locked it up in the Labyrinth, a maze of tunnels he commanded Daedalus to create beneath the royal palace.

The Greeks derived several moral lessons from Pasiphae's disturbing tale, one of which involved the place of ordinary sorcery in nature's greater scheme. The magical abilities possessed by goddesses like Pasiphae and Circe seemed formidable and scary to the average human. Yet these powers paled before those of the much stronger deity Poseidon. In turn, Zeus's supernatural talents outstripped those of the sea god; and even Zeus was defenseless in the face of fate, the cosmos's final arbiter. Therefore, the kind of magic Pasiphae practiced proved ultimately useless, as it could not keep her from bringing everlasting shame on herself and her marriage.

Chapter Five

Fearless Warrior Women

The classical Greeks held a true fascination for warrior women, an attitude that repeatedly appears in myths about Athena and other goddesses who wore armor and fought like male Greek soldiers. Also, most Greek men were haunted by legends of the Amazons, warrior women who supposedly dwelled in the grassy plains lying north of the Black Sea. Each Amazon was said to be a match for a Greek warrior, and Greek mythology is riddled with stories about male heroes fighting off attacks by these forceful, hostile women.

Interestingly, images of such aggressive women were compelling to Greek men, both sexually and intellectually. Yet at the same time, they were repellent because they were seen as decidedly abnormal. The natural question, of course, is why Greek men were so captivated by the idea of ferocious females—a clear paradox, or contradiction in terms. Historian David Sacks makes the point that such women

> were in part a reverse projection of the dowdy, housebound lives of actual Greek women, most of whom were excluded from the men's world, bereft of both political power and sexual freedom. Imaginary "male women" apparently were both fascinating and frightening to Greek men. On the one hand, the Greeks found tall, athletic women generally attractive, and the legend of hard-riding, overtly sexual Amazons seems designed in part to provide an enjoyable male

fantasy. On the other hand, the Amazons represented the kind of foreign, irrational power that was felt to threaten life in the ordered Greek city-state.[37]

Greek writers and artists most often expressed this contradiction between attraction and repulsion for strong women in two principal ways. The first was in the frequently repeated theme of what they called Amazonomachy—fictional, mythical battles with those women. The other was open worship of Athena, Artemis, Nike, and other female deities who presented military, warlike personalities and visual symbols.

Crowned by an Olive Wreath

One of Athena's primary symbols, for example, was the aegis, a supposedly invincible breastplate or shield she wore or carried. (Her other main symbol, the owl, represented her alternate major function—goddess of wisdom.) The aegis stood for her steadfast guardianship of Greece as a whole and Athens in particular. She became that city-state's divine patron and overall champion not long after Greece arose from the cultural devastation of the Dark Age. Moreover, although she did represent all Greeks, many of the popular myths in which she appears concerned Athenian history and issues in particular.

One of those local Athenian tales that all Greeks came to embrace featured another of the goddess's signature symbols—the olive tree. At some point in the dim past, the story went, she flew over Athens and hurled a wooden statue of herself onto the city's central, rocky hill, the Acropolis. The spot the object struck thereafter became the site for a series of temples dedicated to her, each called the Erechtheum. Inside stood the fallen statue, or at least what local priests claimed was that sacred relic. Eventually, only a few feet away from this temple, the Athenians erected a larger one—the magnificent Parthenon. Within its walls stood a 40-foot-tall (12.2 m) statue of Athena created by the great sculptor Phidias.

Athena, whom the Romans called Minerva, is the subject of this nineteenth-century statue made of marble and bronze. Her helmet, shield, and spear symbolized her role as war goddess.

Thanks to artists like Phidias, the Athenians and other Greeks developed a standard idea of what Athena purportedly looked like. The Roman novelist Apuleius captured it for posterity, saying in part, "Her head was covered with a gleaming helmet which was itself crowned with an olive-wreath. She bore a shield and brandished a spear, simulating the goddess's fighting role."[38]

In this impressive military guise, Athena took her stand atop Athens's Acropolis in another of her myths in which that city is the central focus. That tale claims that she early on developed a fondness for Athens and its residents and desired to become its official local patron deity. The trouble was that the sea god Poseidon sought the same honor. So the two Olympians held a public contest that was to be judged by none other than the master of Olympus himself, Zeus. The goal of the competition was to determine which deity could provide the city with something useful to all its inhabitants. According to Pseudo-Apollodorus, "Poseidon was the first that came to [Athens], and with a blow of his trident on the middle of the Acropolis, he produced a [stream] which they now call Erekhtheis. After him came Athena, and, having called on [the city's king] to witness her act of taking possession, she planted an olive tree, which is still shown in [a local shrine]."[39]

Poseidon

The god of the sea

Born in Full Battle Armor

Zeus concluded that Athena's planting of Athens's first olive tree (in some ancient accounts the *world's* first) was the contest's most beneficial long-term feat. So he chose the armor-clad goddess as the competition's victor. From that time on, she was the city's patron deity and, along with several other titles, bore the name Athena Polias, or "Athena of the City."

For her larger role as war goddess for *all* the Greeks, one of Athena's chief myths recounted her miraculous but violent birth. The most often cited ancient Greek account of the event is that of Hesiod in his *Theogony*. But many other Greek writers depicted it, including the third-century-CE orator Philostratus the Elder. In his work *Imagines*, he describes the details of a large painting of Athena's birth located in Naples, a work that tragically was lost over the centuries. Singling out some of the painting's characters, he states:

> These wonder-struck beings are gods and goddesses, for the decree has gone forth that not even the nymphs may leave the heavens, but that [they] must be at hand; and they shudder at the sight of Athena, who at this moment has just burst forth fully armed from the head of Zeus. [As]

for the material of her panoply [armor and weapons], no one could guess it; for as many as are the colors of the rainbow [are] the colors of her armor. Hephaestus [the god who regularly made the gods' armor] seems at a loss to know [how] her armor was born with her. Zeus breathes deeply with delight, like men who have undergone a great contest for a great prize, and he looks searchingly for his daughter, feeling pride in his offspring.[40]

The Greeks Versus the Amazons

Wars and battles between Greeks and Amazons occurred so frequently in Greek mythology that the Greeks coined a special word for such fighting—Amazonomachy. A number of Greek heroes supposedly tangled with the fabulous warrior women, among them the famous strongman Heracles. Among his many renowned accomplishments, he managed to steal the girdle (a wide belt) of the Amazons queen, Hippolyta. A much larger conflict later took place between Hippolyta and the Athenian hero Theseus. The troubles started when he gathered a force of soldiers and entered Amazonian territory, perhaps to conquer part of it. Hearing about this intrusion, Hippolyta sent her younger sister, Antiope, to try to reason with the strangers. But for reasons he never revealed, Theseus arrested Antiope and took her back to Athens.

Hippolyta wasted little time in mounting an invasion of Athens in hopes of freeing her captured sister. Realizing the Amazons were approaching, Theseus ordered his men to form a long battle line. When the great battle was finally joined, his first-century-CE Greek biographer Plutarch wrote, "The Athenians engaged the [enemy's] left wing. [On] this flank, the women routed the Athenians and forced them back, [but] on the other side, the Athenians who attacked the Amazons [pushed] their right wing back to their camp and killed great numbers of them." So many soldiers died on both sides that the Greeks and Amazons decided to make peace, and the warrior women soon returned to their homeland.

Plutarch, *Life of Theseus*, in *The Rise and Fall of Athens: Nine Greek Lives by Plutarch*, trans. Ian Scott-Kilvert. New York: Penguin, 1984, p. 33.

Athena also appears in a number of small-scale myths that trace her continuing involvement in the Trojan War. In the first, she takes part in the Judgment of Paris, in which she and two other goddesses have a contest to see which is the fairest. Athena was disappointed when Troy's Prince Paris chose Aphrodite as the winner. Partly for that reason, the war goddess backed the Greeks during their ten-year siege of the city. In his *Iliad*, Homer described several scenes in which she helped Greek warriors defeat their Trojan adversaries.

In the war's final moments, however, Athena turned against the Greeks. This was because one of the leading Greek warriors—Ajax the Lesser—violated the shrine the Trojans had dedicated to her well before the conflict had begun. He raped a young woman who had entered the shrine to acquire the goddess's protection. In retaliation, the outraged Athena convinced her brother Poseidon to whip up a great storm to scatter the Greek ships on their homeward voyages.

The Winged Goddess of Victory

Although a number of the Greeks who fought at Troy did not reach their homelands as quickly as they would have liked, once home they could report a major victory over the Trojans. Many factors had ensured that success, one of which, the Greeks believed, was the influence of the goddess of victory, Nike. It was said that she was a daughter of the Titan Pallas and that she became one of Zeus's strongest initial supporters. In the massive war between the Titan gods and Zeus's Olympian deities—the so-called Titanomachy—Nike drove Zeus's chariot for him as he hurled thunderbolts at his opponents.

Nike

The goddess of victory

The classical Greeks pictured Nike as Athena's close ally and at times her attendant. This is why the two deities were so often depicted together in Greek paintings and sculptures. The most famous example was the human-sized figure of Nike that stood in the upraised palm of Phidias's giant statue of Athena in the Parthenon. The general belief was that Nike, who had wings, aided the war goddesses by flying over a battlefield and ensuring that the fighters Athena backed were giving it their all.

A modern statue of Athena holds a smaller statue of Nike, goddess of victory. Such depictions are inspired by the giant statue of Athena holding Nike that once stood inside the Parthenon.

Nike became particularly popular during the fifth century BCE, when the mighty Persian Empire twice invaded Greece, inciting some of the most decisive battles in Western history. Perhaps not surprisingly, the Greeks prayed to her more often and more urgently than they ever had. This helped create a refurbished mythical image of her and spawned new hymns and prayers dedicated to her. One of those hymns has survived. Beautifully written, it says in part:

> I call upon you, mighty Nike, beloved of mortals. She alone frees men from the eagerness for contest, from dissent, when men face each other in battle. In war, you are the judge of deeds deserving prizes. Sweet is the boast you grant after the onslaught [attack]. Nike, mistress of all, on your good name depends noble glory, glory that comes from the strife and teems with festivities. O blessed and beloved one, come with joy in your eyes, come for the works of renown, [and] bring me noble glory.[41]

Swift and Terrifying Vengeance

Both Nike and Athena projected images in ancient Greek religion as traditional warriors—essentially, female versions of male military figures. Another goddess, Nemesis, was not seen as a conventional military figure yet was no less capable of wielding impressive power and of striking fear into human hearts. Her chief role was to maintain a balance between happiness and unhappiness in nature and human affairs. More often than not, this entailed her stepping in and disciplining individuals guilty of excessive pride or of abusing whatever power and authority they held.

Thus, Nemesis was sometimes an avenging deity who meted out punishment to criminals, corrupt rulers, heartless lovers, and other human transgressors. Moreover, her vengeance could be swift and terrifying. One example of Nemesis's wrath

Aura
A minor goddess of breezes

was her punishment of the minor virgin goddess Aura, who oversaw cool breezes. One day Aura unwisely criticized Artemis, goddess of hunting, who was also famed for being a lifelong virgin. Arrogantly, Aura claimed that Artemis was not really a virgin, whereas Aura herself *was*.

Upset, Artemis hurried to Nemesis and told her what had happened. Immediately, the deity of retribution saw that Aura's excessive pride and mean spirit could not be allowed to stand. She took Artemis by the hand, and the two mounted a chariot. Nemesis told Artemis (according to the fifth-century-CE Greek writer Nonnus) that Aura "shall be a virgin no longer. You shall see her in the bed of a mountain stream weeping fountains of tears for her maiden girdle."[42]

After a wild ride over mountains and through forests, the chariot arrived in the place where Aura dwelled. Her face contorted into a mask of fury, Nemesis "approached haughty Aura," Nonnus continued. "She flicked the proud neck of the hapless girl with her snaky whip, and struck her with the round wheel of justice."[43] That justice consisted of robbing the offending party of her virginity by having the god Dionysus rape her. After this, Aura's unwarranted pride crumbled. She went half mad, and when the baby Dionysus had implanted in her was born, she devoured it.

This episode and others like it convinced the classical Greeks that Nemesis was not a divinity to be trifled with. In a hymn composed to honor her, the writers called her "much revered, of boundless sight, alone rejoicing in the just and right." This indicated that although her punishments were often extremely harsh, most people saw them as a needed form of divine justice. Respect for her was based not only on her role as an equalizer, however, but also on the naked fact that she was a frightening figure. She could literally look inside a person's mind and read his or her thoughts, the hymn emphasized: "For every thought within the mind concealed is to your sight plainly revealed."[44]

The Divine Huntress

Exactly why Artemis sought Nemesis's help regarding Aura's insult is unclear. The Greeks never claimed that the characters and events of their myths were either consistent or logical. It may be that whoever originated this myth chose Artemis as the injured party mainly because she was known to be a virgin, like Aura herself.

In any case, a number of other myths demonstrate that Artemis was every bit as formidable a female deity as Nemesis was. Artemis was the twin sister of Apollo, both children of the

Artemis, whom the Romans called Diana, is seen in this copy of an ancient Greek painting. She bears her trusty bow and is accompanied by two hunting dogs, a reminder that she oversaw animal hunts.

Titan goddess Leto. The Greeks revered Artemis as the goddess of hunting, wild places, and the untamed beasts that inhabited those places. She was often depicted as an expert archer, as well as a fearsome fighter with other weapons. An ancient hymn to her says in part:

> I sing of Artemis whose shafts [arrows] are of gold, strong-voiced, the revered virgin, arrow-shooting, delighter in arrows, sister to Apollo of the golden sword. Over the shadowy hills and windy peaks she draws her golden bow, rejoicing in the chase, and sends out grievous shafts. The tops of the high mountains tremble and the tangled wood echoes awesomely with the outcry of beasts.[45]

Like most children, whether divine or human, Artemis dearly loved and felt protective of her mother. The divine huntress was outraged, therefore, when she learned that Leto had been horribly insulted by a Theban woman named Niobe. The latter, to her credit, had seven sons and seven daughters, all of them attractive and worthy of a mother's pride. Regrettably, however, she also possessed a streak of arrogance that tainted her character. In a decidedly reckless move, she entered Leto's temple in Thebes and loudly defamed that deity, saying that she, Niobe, was more admirable than Leto because she had fourteen offspring, whereas Leto had only two.

Niobe

A woman who was harshly punished for insulting the goddess Leto

Most local Thebans saw this display as a grave offense. When Leto learned of the incident, she told Artemis, who in her turn informed Apollo. Springing into action, the divine twins gathered their weapons and swooped downward from Olympus's summit. Reaching Thebes in mere minutes, they quickly found Niobe's fourteen children and attacked them without mercy. First, they

Cultural Connections: Athena

Western culture, both ancient and modern, is filled with artistic, literary, and other references to the Greek war goddess Athena. The splendid Parthenon temple, completed in the late 500s BCE on Athens's Acropolis—including its enormous statue of her—was the most famous ancient cultural connection to her. The Greek traveler Pausanias saw the temple and statue a few centuries after they were created and raved about their beauty. "The statue of Athena," he wrote, "stands upright in an ankle-length tunic with the head of [the monster] Medusa carved in ivory on her breast." In late ancient times and the early medieval era, Athena lived on, in a sense, through her incorporation by early Christians into visual images of the Virgin Mary. The earliest versions of those images showed Mary as a warrior maiden who fought with a spear, just as Athena did. More peaceful images of Mary later replaced the warlike ones. Later, during Europe's Renaissance and well beyond, numerous great painters portrayed Athena, among them Sandro Botticelli, Andrea Mantegna, and Peter Paul Rubens.

Modern statues of the goddess also appeared across Europe and the United States. These include an ornate sculpture, completed in the 1880s in front of Austria's parliament building in Vienna. They also include a towering statue of the goddess inside the exact replica of the Parthenon erected in Nashville, Tennessee, for the 1897 Tennessee Centennial Exposition.

Pausanias, *Guide to Greece*, vol. 1, trans. Peter Levi. New York: Penguin, 1984, p. 69.

slew the seven brothers, then turned on their seven sisters. In Ovid's words:

> The twang of the [divine] bowstrings rang out, bringing terror. The sisters [stood] where their brothers lay in death. One, as she pulled the arrow from his flesh, fell dying as she tried to kiss her brother's lips. A second, endeavoring to console her mother in her misery suddenly fell silent and doubled up with a hidden wound. One sank down as she tried in vain to

escape. [After] six had been taken by death, [Niobe], shielding [her] last child with her [body], cried out, "Leave this one for me, leave me the youngest one! [I] pray you!" But even as she prayed, the one she [tried] to save fell dead.[46]

Niobe had learned a lesson in humility the hard way. Meanwhile, from this and other similar myths the classical Greeks grew up with, they absorbed that lesson. In Greek culture, respect for the immortals who governed the cosmos was paramount and expected. Moreover, humans were likely to pay a heavy price for disrespecting those divine beings. The female deities seemed even more concerned with their reputations and honor than the male ones. Perhaps that was because the goddesses realized they would never be equal to the patriarchal Zeus and resented that inequality. Whatever the reason, the goddesses were moved most by "considerations of personal honor," as C.M. Bowra put it. "Forgiveness was not in their nature, and once a human had offended them, he had no excuse and could expect no mercy."[46]

Source Notes

Introduction: Myths as Mangled Memories

1. C.M. Bowra, *The Greek Experience*. New York: Barnes & Noble, 1996, p. 32.
2. Michael Grant, *The Rise of the Greeks*. New York: Scribner's, 2006, p. 17.
3. Pindar, *Sixth Nemean Ode*, in *Pindar: The Odes*, trans. C.M. Bowra. New York: Penguin, 1985, p. 206.
4. Evy J. Haland, "Women, Death, and the Body in Some of Plutarch's Writings," *Mediterranean Review*, December 2011, p. 41.

Chapter One: Guardians of Nature's Realm

5. *Homeric Hymn to Athena*, in *Hesiod, the Homeric Hymns, and Homerica*, trans. Hugh G. Evelyn-White. Cambridge, MA: Harvard University Press, 1964, pp. 453, 455.
6. *Homeric Hymn to Aphrodite*, in *Hesiod, the Homeric Hymns, and Homerica*, trans. Hugh G. Evelyn-White. Cambridge, MA: Harvard University Press, 1964, p. 409.
7. *Homeric Hymn to Hestia*, in *Hesiod, the Homeric Hymns, and Homerica*, trans. Hugh G. Evelyn-White. Cambridge, MA: Harvard University Press, 1964, p. 455.
8. *Homeric Hymn to Aphrodite*, p. 409.
9. Homer, *Iliad*, trans. W.H.D. Rouse. New York: Signet, 2015, p. 228.
10. Edith Hamilton, *Mythology*. New York: Grand Central, 2011, p. 290.
11. Apollonius, *Argonautica*, published as *Apollonius of Rhodes, The Voyage of the Argo*, trans. E.V. Rieu. New York: Penguin, 1971, p. 80.
12. Apollonius, *Argonautica*, p. 81.
13. Quoted in Theoi Greek Mythology, "Hesperides." www.theoi.com.

Chapter Two: Mother Figures and Women's Protectors

14. Eva Cantarella, *Pandora's Daughters: The Role and Status of Women in Greek and Roman Antiquity*. Baltimore: Johns Hopkins University Press, 1987, p. 14.
15. Hesiod, *Theogony*, in *Hesiod and Theognis*, trans. Dorothea Wender. New York: Penguin, 1982, p. 24.
16. *Orphic Hymn to Hera*, in *The Mystical Hymns of Orpheus*, trans. Thomas Taylor. London: Bertrand Dobell, 1896, p. 50.
17. Ovid, *Metamorphoses*, trans. Rolfe Humphries. Bloomington: Indiana University Press, 1967, pp. 93–94.
18. Homer, *Iliad*, trans. Richmond Lattimore. Chicago: University of Chicago Press, 1963, p. 241.
19. Pindar, *Seventh Nemean Ode*, in *Pindar: The Odes*, trans. C.M. Bowra. New York: Penguin, 1985, p. 158.

Chapter Three: Lovers and Patrons of the Arts

20. Thomas Craven, *Greek Art*. New York: Pocket, 1950, pp. 36–37.
21. *Homeric Hymn to Aphrodite*, p. 427.
22. Quoted in Theoi Greek Mythology, "Tyche." www.theoi.com.
23. Aesop, "The Traveler and Fortune," in *Aesop's Fables*, trans. George F. Townsend, Internet Classics Archive. http://classics.mit.edu.
24. Edith Hamilton, *The Greek Way to Western Civilization*. New York: Norton, 1993, p. 25.
25. Pindar, *Fourteenth Olympian Ode*, in *Pindar: The Odes*, trans. C.M. Bowra. New York: Penguin, 1985, p. 32.
26. Pindar, *Ninth Olympian Ode*, in *Pindar: The Odes*, trans. C.M. Bowra. New York: Penguin, 1985, pp. 152–53.
27. Hesiod, *Theogony*, p. 26.
28. *Homeric Hymn to Apollo*, in *Hesiod, the Homeric Hymns, and Homerica*, trans. Hugh G. Evelyn-White. Cambridge, MA: Harvard University Press, 1964, pp. 337, 339.
29. Homer, *Odyssey*, trans. E.V. Rieu. New York: Penguin, 2003, p. 352.
30. Hamilton, *The Greek Way to Western Civilization,* p. 26.

Chapter Four: Those Who Deal in Prophecy and Sorcery

31. Aeschylus, *Prometheus Bound*, trans. Philip Vellacott, in *Aeschylus: Prometheus Bound, The Suppliants, Seven Against Thebes, The Persians*. New York: Penguin, 1986, p. 27.
32. Quintus Smyrnaeus, *The Fall of Troy*, trans. Arthur S. Way. New York: William Heinemann, 1913, p. 449.
33. Ovid, *Metamorphoses*, trans. Mary M. Innes. London: Penguin, 2006, p. 318.
34. Homer, *Odyssey*, pp. 168–70.
35. Euripides, *Medea*, in *Euripides: Medea and Other Plays*, trans. Philip Vellacott. London: Penguin, 1984, p. 29.
36. Quoted in Theoi Greek Mythology, "Pasiphae." www.theoi.com.

Chapter Five: Fearless Warrior Women

37. David Sacks, *Encyclopedia of the Ancient Greek World*. New York: Facts On File, 1995, p. 19.
38. Apuleius, *The Golden Ass*, trans. P.G. Walsh. New York: Oxford University Press, 1995, p. 213.
39. Quoted in Theoi Greek Mythology, "Athena Myths 1." www.theoi.com.
40. Philostratus the Elder, *Imagines*, trans. Arthur Fairbanks. Cambridge, MA: Harvard University Press, 1931, pp. 245, 247.
41. Quoted in Apostolos N. Athanassakis and Benjamin M. Wolkow, trans. and eds., "The Orphic Hymns." Baltimore: Johns Hopkins University, 2013, pp. 29–30.
42. Quoted in Theoi Greek Mythology, "Aura." www.theoi.com.
43. Quoted in Theoi Greek Mythology, "Aura."
44. Quoted in Theoi Greek Mythology, "Nemesis." www.theoi.com.
45. *Homeric Hymn to Artemis*, in *Hesiod, the Homeric Hymns, and Homerica*, trans. Hugh G. Evelyn-White. Cambridge, MA: Harvard University Press, 1964, p. 453.
46. Ovid, *Metamorphoses*, in *Classical Gods and Heroes: Myths as Told by the Ancient Authors*, trans. Rhoda A. Hendricks. New York: Morrow Quill, 1978, pp. 79–80.
47. Bowra, *The Greek Experience*, p. 63.

The Ancient Myth Tellers

Aeschylus

Today often called the world's first great playwright, he was born around 525 BCE. In 490 BCE, when in his thirties, he fought in the pivotal battles of Marathon and Salamis, both against Persian invaders. All of his more than eighty plays (seven of which survive) were heavily influenced by the huge corpus of old Greek myths, parts of which he dramatized in those works.

Euripides

Born in about 485 BCE, this Athenian master of tragic drama wrote more than eighty plays, nineteen of which have survived. He was known for his frequent emphasis of themes and ideas that questioned traditional religious and social values. Among his works that retell important Greek myths are *Alcestis* (438 BCE), *Medea* (431), *Electra* (ca. 413–417), and *Helen* (412).

Herodotus

Often considered the father of history because he wrote the first-known modern-style history text, he was born around 484 BCE. Although he dealt largely with historical events, his book mentions or summarizes a number of old Greek myths. They include episodes and characters from the Trojan War, Theseus and the Minotaur, and Zeus's disguising himself as a bull.

Hesiod

Born sometime during the early 700s BCE, the ancient Greeks considered him one of the two greatest epic poets (the other being Homer). Hesiod was a farmer by trade but devoted much of his time to writing. His two epic poems, *Works and Days* and the *Theogony*, contain a wealth of detail about the early Greek creation myths, including the rise of the first race of gods, the Titans.

Homer

His birth year is unknown, but he likely lived during the 700s BCE. One of several storytellers, called bards, who recited long narratives in public, it appears that he created the final versions of the already existing epics the *Iliad* and the *Odyssey*. For the Greeks, these works, containing many dozens of myths large and small, were crucial sources of their moral codes and social and political attitudes.

Ovid

Publius Ovidius Naso (43 BCE–17 CE), popularly known as Ovid, was one of Rome's finest poets. One of his books, titled the *Metamorphoses*, contains his own retellings of a majority of the important ancient Greek myths. This collection of tales survived Rome's fall and became more popular than ever during medieval times and the early modern era.

Plutarch

A pivotal and widely popular Greek biographer and moralist, he was born in about 46 CE. He is best known for two massive literary works—*Parallel Lives*, consisting of fifty detailed biographies of well-known Greek and Roman military and political figures, and *Moralia*, a collection of absorbing essays on moral, political, philosophical, and other issues. Both works feature references to the traditional Greek myths.

Pseudo-Apollodorus

His real name is unknown and modern experts call him Pseudo-Apollodorus, meaning the "fake Apollodorus." Whoever he was, he likely lived during the first century CE or somewhat later. What is more certain is that his masterwork, often called the *Bibliotheca*, or *Library*, is the largest single compilation of Greek myths penned in the ancient world. If this work had not survived, numerous Greek myths would have been tragically lost to humanity and today be unknown.

For Further Research

Books

Apollonius of Rhodes, *Argonautica*, trans. Aaron Poochigian. New York: Penguin, 2014.

Jane Bingham, *Classical Myth: A Treasury of Greek and Roman Legends, Art, and History*. London: Routledge, 2016.

Mike Clayton, *Greek Mythology: A Captivating Guide to the Ancient Gods, Goddesses, Heroes, and Monsters*. Charleston, SC: Amazon Digital Services, 2017.

Edith Hamilton, *Mythology*. New York: Grand Central, 2011.

Sarah I. Johnston, *The Story of Myth*. Cambridge, MA: Harvard University Press, 2018.

Oliver Laine, *Greek Mythology*. Charleston, SC: Amazon Digital Services, 2017.

Liam Saxon, *A Smart Kids Guide to Ancient Greek Gods and Goddesses*. New York: Create Space, 2015.

Katerina Servi, *Greek Mythology: Gods & Heroes: The Trojan War and the Odyssey*. Baton Rouge, LA: Third Millennium, 2018.

Internet Sources

Mike Belmont, "Poseidon: Greek God of the Sea," Gods and Monsters.com. www.gods-and-monsters.com.

N.S. Gill, "Prometheus: Fire Bringer and Philanthropist," ThoughtCo., March 6, 2017. www.thoughtco.com.

Manfred Korfmann, "Was There a Trojan War?," *Archaeology*, 2018. http://archive.archaeology.org.

Sabine McKellen, "Why Were Women a Necessary Evil in Greek Mythology?," Classroom. http://classroom.synonym.com.

Vera Norman, "Four Conceptions of the Heroic," Fellowship of Reason. www.fellowshipofreason.com.

Nick Romeo, "The Gods of Olympus," *Christian Science Monitor*, March 12, 2014. www.csmonitor.com.

Websites

Greek Mythology Link (www.maicar.com). This well-thought-out site has a biographical dictionary with more than six thousand entries and some forty-five hundred photos, drawings, and other images.

Mythweb Encyclopedia of Greek Mythology (www.mythweb .com/encyc). Although not as comprehensive and detailed as the Theoi Greek Mythology site (see below), this website provides a lot of useful information about both major and minor Greek mythological characters.

Theoi Greek Mythology (www.theoi.com). This is the most comprehensive and reliable general website about Greek mythology on the internet. It features hundreds of separate pages filled with detailed, accurate information, as well as numerous primary sources and reproductions of ancient paintings and mosaics.

Index

Picture Credits

Cover: babin/Shutterstock.com

6: Maury Aaseng

11: Vase with scene of assembly of gods: Zeus, Ganymede and Vesta, Detail of Vesta/De Agostini Picture Library/G. Dagli Orti/Bridgeman Images

15: Aurora quitting Tithonus in her Chariot (after Guercino), English School, (18th century)/Powis Castle, Wales, UK/National Trust Photographic Library/Bridgeman Images

18: Fine Art Images/Newscom

24: Pictures From History/Newscom

27: Semele is Deceived or Semele Ingannata da Giunone, illustration from Ovid's Metamorphoses, Florence, 1832 (hand-coloured engraving), Ademollo, Luigi (1764–1849)/Private Collection/The Stapleton Collection/Bridgeman Images

30: Florilegius/Newscom

35: The Birth of Venus, c.1485 (tempera on canvas), Botticelli, Sandro (Alessandro di Mariano di Vanni Filipepi) (1444/5–1510)/Galleria degli Uffizi, Florence, Tuscany, Italy/Bridgeman Images

39: Primavera, c.1478, (tempera on panel), Botticelli, Sandro (Alessandro di Mariano di Vanni Filipepi) (1444/5–1510)/Galleria degli Uffizi, Florence, Tuscany, Italy/Bridgeman Images

42: Erato, Muse of Lyrical Poetry, 1800 (oil on canvas) , Meynier, Charles (1768–1832)/Cleveland Museum of Art, OH, USA/Severance and Greta Millikin Purchase Fund/Bridgeman Images

46: World History Archive/Newscom

49: Circe Offering the Cup to Ulysses, 1891 (oil on canvas), Waterhouse, John William (1849–1917)/Gallery Oldham, UK/Bridgeman Images

52: Jason and Medea, 1907 (oil on canvas), Waterhouse, John William (1849–1917)/Private Collection/Photo © The Maas Gallery, London/Bridgeman Images

58: Minerva by Pierre Charles Simart (1806–57), 1855 (bronze and marble)/Chateau de Duc de Luynes, Dampierre, France/Peter Willi/Bridgeman Images

62: vladacanon/iStockphoto.com

65: Hoika Mikhail/Shutterstock.com